···Gemini VI···

Tamela (Devine) Carrington

Gemini VI

© 2021 by Tamela "Devine" Carrington
All rights reserved.

No part of this book may be reproduced, distributed, utilized, or transmitted in any form or by any means, including, photocopying, and internet usage, without written permission of the copyright owner, or publisher except for the use of brief quotations in a book review. For permissions contact - ascensionpublishingllc@gmail.com

Disclaimer
This book is a work of fiction, although it is inspired from real life incidents. Names characters, places, and events are either the products of the author's imagination or used in a fictious manner. Any resemblance or similarity to real persons, living or dead, are purely coincidental.

Cover Design by Julius Chatters
Cover Photography by Julius Chatters
Interior Design by Christopher Allen
Edited by Christopher Allen

Ascension Publishing, LLC
P.O. Box 1501
Midlothian, VA 23113

Library of Congress Catalog Number: 2022907945

ISBN: 978-1-7367803-3-6 (Paperback)
ASIN: B09-Z-MWFVK- (E-book)

Autobiography   Poetry

PRINTED IN THE UNITED STATES OF AMERICA

PREFACE

Have you ever felt alone, misunderstood, or stuck in bondage? I'm here to take you on a mental journey through my eyes, mind, and soul. Revealing my trials and tribulations of being uniquely different as a child. I've learned how to express myself creatively though art and poetry. Bullying, domestic, and sexual abuse was very real in my early years. Because of it, I'm now living and coping with PTSD, depression, and early Alzheimer's disease. Throughout this book original poems that were written during those times in my life are shared. As a survivor, I am still here to share my testimonies. This is my journey of strength and healing. Welcome to my story of written therapy!

GEMINI VI

BEGINNING

Precious Lord

Take my hand and lead me

And not let me stray

I am tired

I am weak

I am worn, through the storm

And through the night

Lead me to the light

Take my hand, precious Lord

Lead me home

GEMINI- THE TWIN

We are the ruler of Mercury,
perfectly mutable, air sign

ACKNOWLEDGEMENT

A Special thank you to all my family and friends that got a chance to know my many personalities. Thank you to my mother Lillian for always believing in me and pushing me when I didn't believe in myself.

To my daughter and twin, JaShaya, I love you so much! Thank you and your brother Je'Hario for listening to all my late-night stories. I love you both.

To my sisters, brother, and bestie, thank you for being in my life, although I am the oldest, LOL!

To all my cousins, aunts, uncles, mentors, and friends, thank you for playing a part in my life as well. Maria thank you for loving me and excepting all six of me. Thank you, Chris, for being awesome and being there every step of the way! Thank you, Julius, for capturing the perfect cover of me to tell my story! Without you and most of all God, it would not have been possible. If you are reading this, thank you, thank you, thank you!!!

In loving memory of my Papa (Robert), Granny (Carrie), Aunty Shorty (Carolyn) and my daddy (Harrell), their love was never unwavering!

INTRODUCTION

Every time I close my eyes, I see that goat! Running up the outside stairs banging his head into the bottom of the door over and over again! So, I asked mom, "Do you guys have a pet goat?"

Mom says, "No!"

So, I ask my Granny, "Do we have a goat?"

Granny says, "No, baby!"

I say to myself, I know I am not crazy. I have been having this dream all of my life, laughing out loud. I am only at the ripe age of ten, but when I turned eighteen, I revisited this same question again with my Granny.

I asked, "Granny did you all ever have a goat?"

Finally, my Granny says, "Yes, baby we did about fifteen years before I was born."

In total shock I said, "Wait! What? Fifteen years before I was born! How is that possible for me to even know that?" So, I asked my Granny, "Why all these years was I lead to believe it was untrue?"

My Granny responded, "I didn't want to scare you because you were not born yet!"

Shocked, I asked, "But how?"

Granny looked me in the eyes and said, "But God, we are all different and God gives us all gifts and now you know one of yours…. pay attention!"

CONTENTS

PREFACE	4
BEGINNING	5
GEMINI- THE TWIN	6
ACKNOWLEDGEMENT	7
INTRODUCTION	8
CONTENTS	11
CHAPTER 1	14
I DIDN'T DO ANYTHING	18
CHAPTER 2	20
MY OTHER SIDE	21
CHAPTER 3	23
ATTENTION	24
SOLDIERS	26
CHAPTER 4	27
A WAITING	30
CHAPTER 5	31
FAIRYTALE	34
CHAPTER 6	35
GEMINI	38
CHAPTER 7	39
BROKEN GLASS	44
CHAPTER 8	45
SUICIDE	50
RAGE	51

WANTING LOVE	52
CHAPTER 9	54
PTSD	57
CHAPTER 10	58
AWAKENING	62
BONUS POEMS	64
A WHISPER	64
HUE	65
HYPOCRITES	66
DAUGHTER	67
RACE	68
DO YOU SEE ME	69
AUTHENTICLY ME	70
MY SINCERE ADVICE	83

CHAPTER I

I always knew I was a little different from the rest of my family. It started when I would just embrace the stillness around me. Like I would find the prettiest rock and keep it as a gift or the most unique pinecone or stick, anything that looked beautiful, but singled out at the same time. I guess it made me feel safe because I felt like we had something in common. I was a good kid. At least I thought so. I got good grades, played sports, stayed out of trouble and just kind of did what I was supposed to do and stayed out of the way.

I was definitely sheltered and spoiled with love. I learned by the age of seven what being an introvert was like. My toys became my friends. Just like any other child would do back in the day. But when it came to school that was another story. I was very shy. If I knew the answer in class, I dare not answer out loud. I am silently praying, please don't pick me. Please don't! Guess what? You guessed it the teacher picked me. I felt like I was about to pass out because I have to speak in front of the class. They are all going to laugh at me and tease me like they always do. I gave the wrong answer because I was so nervous although I knew the right answer. The kids snickered at me and from there it got worse, "Hey blacky, you are so skinny! You look like Olive Oil. Why do you look like the Buck Tooth Beaver?"

I would go home into my room and cry. I would ask myself, "Why me? What's wrong with me?" That was when I started to feel different emotions and noticing my thoughts were deep, heavy, and very artistic. I found out that I actually enjoyed everything about the arts, drawing, writing dancing, and creating, I loved it all. It was exciting and I was actually good at it. I was more of the tomboy type as a little kid. Lol! I had Barbie Dolls, but I also had Transformers, action figures and BB Guns. I never been into the really girly thing, but I'd play Dodge Ball, Flag Football, and Hide and Go Seek. I was the first one in line to play. As I stated before my childhood for the most part was very loving.

I was taught about the simple things not the material things. The value of things was so much better back then. As I got older it became more noticeable to me that I was different.

    I remember I was learning to dance. I loved to dance. Back then it was all about Michael Jackson, Madonna, and Whitney Houston. I wanted to go to dance school so bad, but my mom could not afford it. I started watching videos every day and I would practice and practice until one day after my seventh birthday I received an original Michael Jackson Jacket. And glove. I was the happiest kid in the world. I became Michael Jackson and would dance for block parties. I also danced at my aunt's wedding. Dancing made me feel so free. You can just let go and move with the beat.

    My mother moved around a lot, so I had to adjust to whatever school that I attended. Which was sometimes difficult. I actually attended thirteen schools by the time I graduated at the age of seventeen. Sorry, I don't want to get to far ahead, but I remember when the bullying started for me. I was in the 2nd or 3rd grade.

The students teased me saying, "Hey, skinny minnie, why are you here? Hey new girl, go back to Virginia! Hey, blackie, why are you so dark?"

Every day I would go home and look in my mirror and cry. My mother began to take notice that I was becoming more withdrawn. So, one day she said to me, "Baby girl, you are beautiful. Tell yourself every day that you are beautiful. Always remember that! Never let anyone tell you different!" I wanted to believe her, but I just couldn't. It didn't make sense to me. How can I be beautiful and then get called names at the same time? I was at the playground one day and some other kids were there being bad. They were sticking their middle fingers up at cars riding past and just acting grown. Well of course, I saw adults raise their middle fingers all the time. I dismissed the bad kids and went home. Later that day I remember being lectured and put on punishment because someone told my mom that

I was sticking my middle finger up at cars passing by. I was so mad that I started crying and pleading that it wasn't me. I told my mom it was the other kids at the playground. My mother believed me, but I still had one day of punishment. I didn't understand why, but when my mom looked at me, I saw sadness in her eyes and at that moment it didn't matter anymore. That was the day I wrote my first poem and had it published.

I DIDN'T DO ANYTHING

I try to be good

But I guess I should, but

I didn't do anything

No matter what I do

There's no proof

I didn't do anything

Hey, I'm 14, not 14 months, 4 or even 41 years old

I didn't do anything

I might talk to boys

I might even smile at boys

But I did not do anything

When I turned 17 and go to college

I won't doing anything
Well, that's my life and
I didn't do anything

CHAPTER II

One day I was over my aunt's house and my best friend at the time was doing tattoos. I had never seen anyone do a tattoo before, so I was intrigued by the whole process. So of course, me being me, I wanted one. I didn't know what to get so I got a tattoo of my name. At first, I was nervous, but when she started sticking me with the needle. There was a since of pleasure and pain at the same time. A feeling that I enjoyed and especially in a form of art. It was the beginning of my tattoo journey and my pleasure and pain fetish. I was never one into trying to stand out I just wanted to fit in. I recall my mom introducing me to a man named Mr. Wells. He was very handsome and poised for an older man. He had the most beautiful models I had ever seen. They walked with so much confidence, style and grace. I thought, if only I had that confidence. My mom also introduced me to a lady named Ms. Betty and Ms. Carlisa. They became my mentors that day and I instantly fell in love with modeling. I will never forget my very first show.

It was a black and white affair. I walked to a rendition of Natalie Cole and her father, Nat King Cole's *Unforgettable*. It was such an amazing feeling. The beginning of my modeling career had started at the age of 15. Later that year I went on to win Miss Hopewell High. Another huge accomplishment at that time the school was mostly white, and I was one of the first Afro-American women to hold the title Miss Hopewell High.

MY OTHER SIDE

What do you do when you are me?
When you feel like you have died and
You're walking through eternity
I knew I was different in a blessing type of way but,
My brain hurts every breathing day
If only the world knew how I think and feel
They would confuse themselves
Trying to figure out if I'm real
There are two sides to every story
There are two sides to every glory
There are two sides to every place
There are two sides to your face

The birds are chirping so that's my calling
I'll talk again tonight when my eyes start falling

    Why are you so different? Why are you so weird? I would be rich by now for every time I heard this. Now they say you are so unique or mysterious, lol! I never understood why I was so much different than my peers. A lot of the times I would just stay in my room and be in my own world. I learned that I would fall into the always doing what was expected of me instead of doing what I wanted to do like getting good grades and not getting in trouble. I was just trying to be as perfect as I can be. That was a gift and a curse. Winning Mis. Hopewell High was a wonderful achievement for me, but I knew that wasn't enough. I needed more. I needed to see more, do more, so I did the unthinkable.

CHAPTER III

March 1995, I entered the United States Army. That was the most amazing feeling ever. I felt free, confident, ready to defend my country and be all I can be. LOL, I know that sounds cliché, but it was true. I never forgot the look on my mother's face when I told her I had joined. There was a look of shock and to some degree sadness, but I generally knew she was proud as well. I was so excited about training, learning my weapon, you name it. There was nothing that I was afraid of. Well maybe one thing, and that was propelling off the wall. I was super afraid of heights, but I did it. Just like my childhood, I did what was expected of me in the military. I was that gung-ho soldier. I had spit shined boots, stayed physically fit, and was always ready for whatever mission. LOL, I'm always ready for full battle rattle is what we used to say. Throughout my military career I did several fashion and hair shows. LOL, I always made things fashionable even in my uniform going to the gas chamber, staying in the field, and qualifying my

M16 which I was a sharpshooter. Those were small highlights of my day. I lived for the action. I was definitely in my element and then one day it all changed.

ATTENTION

The glint in your eyes

Cannot be disguised

Cover yourself with your own torment

Protect your thoughts

Don't play with the maze

But so often I've lost you in a gaze

No pity party, no self-inflicted pain

Stay above water and feel no shame

Kick one habit and there is another to tame

Release the heat period

End of game

One day, while on a military mission, I ran into the most handsome man with the most amazing smile and the most wildest laugh I have ever heard. We were in the same unit and platoon. Our first date was in the field, LOL! They tied our sleeping bags together as a prank. It was funny, but we both fell trying to get up. LOL! WE were together for 4 months before he asked me to marry him. I was completely shocked.

I said, "Yes!"

We were stationed in Fort Hood, Texas. We had no family here at the time. On February 16th ,1996 I married my first husband at the Justice of the Peace. Things were wonderful in the very beginning. I actually found out a month later that I was actually pregnant with my first child when I got married and I didn't know. Talk about a big surprise. My husband was shocked at the news as well So much so that he made himself a drink. So now I am a soldier who is pregnant and married to another soldier.

SOLDIERS

The life of a soldier is no more
He comes to you to open the door
A ripple effect is flowing through our blood, but
What can you do
Instead of laying 6 feet in the mud?
A diary of tales, a flow chart of notes
The good, the bad, and ugly
That's what the mask man wrote, but
This is realistic and you just been told.

I enjoyed being a soldier it was like it was meant for me but being that I was Dual military which means that both parents are serving in the United States Army and we both couldn't go to war at the same time because there are children involved. So, we made the decision that I would get out and be a housewife. Me being a housewife., LOL! This only lasted for about 30 days. Those were the quiet times before the storms, before the name calling, before the fights, physical contact, the jealousy, the mental torture of being belittled

CHAPTER IV

I never thought marriage for me would be this way. Lies, betrayal, pain, hurt, night terrors, crying myself to sleep, hiding, and running. Why me Lord? I would cry out what did I do to deserve such torment. I would never forget the look in my children's eyes at an early age. I felt so small and defeated. I didn't know what to do so for a while I did nothing and just took the abuse. I started modeling again to have some sort of outlet. I would take my kids with me to practice sometimes because I didn't have anyone to help me. At this time, we were stationed Fort Hood, Texas. The four walls were closing in on me. I'm feeling stuck, and I would hear in my head, what can I do? Who can help me? Where can I go? I also heard in my head enough is enough! When do you truly know you had enough? Restless night, swollen eyes, from crying, prayer after prayer asking God to help me, save me! The only way out that I could see was to leave this world. Yes, death seems like the only option that made sense. I've tried pills on several occasions with no luck. I tried jumping out of a window and yes, I did try that with no luck. I tried cutting my wrist and no luck there either. Whatever I tried did not work so I knew my plan was definitely not God's plan, but there was definitely time for a change. I knew I had to change my way of thinking and change my heart. I was a veteran now and no longer on active duty. I had to do something to get out of this bondage. If I couldn't save myself, I had to save my children. They needed to be surrounded by love and peace, especially after they saw me being mentally and physically abused. What they saw was not healthy. The very thing that broke the Camel's back was our last altercation. It turned into five Police cars arriving at our home, him being maced twice, and I filed a restraining order against him. I had enough. It was time to go! I am a survivor and a fighter. I would say to myself, I had to give my kids a fair chance at life. A few weeks later I made a few phone calls. The time had come, and I packed up my kids and dog. My mother flew into town to help me drive leaving Texas, the pain I endured, behind. I was heading to Virginia for a fresh start. Yes, a fresh start is what my kids and I needed.

A WAITING

You cheated, you lied, you played me like a fool
You abused me mentally and
Physically like I was your tool
My scalp has bled
Ankles twisted and face swollen
All because your wanted to control me
I went through the neglect, the disrespect, and being
taken advantage of day by day
I wondered why I stayed
How can you love
When can't you remember one thing to the next?
How can you love when you have no regret?
I'm not a beauty queen or a two-bit whore
But to Some calmly person, they will simply adore
Everyone has baggage that they carry in their lives
But it takes a strong person to know how to divide
So, do the impossible and change your evil ways
Because if you, don't you all have limited days
One day I will wake up and be able to see and realize
The life that I have isn't meant for me
Until that day comes my eyes will stay closed
And I will
Keep hoping that God will deliver me
Like a beautiful red rose

CHAPTER V

Living in Virginia, definitively had its ups and downs. The southern hospitality can sometimes be warming, but the weather can have you feeling a little confused. It was quite an adjustment for us even our Doberman, Dutchess, had to adjust. In hindsight, this was the safest place to live for my children. Feeling broken, defeated and alone, I was starting another chapter in my life. Everything was going well at least I wanted to believe that it was. I started working at the local restaurant in the town I lived in. I actually applied for the assistant manager position before I moved to Virginia. My children were adjusting to their new school environment. In Texas, they had to wear a uniform to school and in Virginia you could wear anything you wanted. That was quite an adjustment. It was nice to be around family and have support. I think back to when I was in Germany. I never felt so trapped. Don't get me wrong, the country was very beautiful, clean and the people were polite, but I had no family there. I was alone. I was with my husband, but I was truly alone.

There were a lot of domestic issues, suicide attempts and just feeling like I had no one. But now I am back in Virginia, my hometown trying to start a new life. Even though I was home and around family I was somewhat a stranger. I wasn't that same little girl that I was before I went into the military. Sometimes it was hard to relate. In fact, it was very hard to relate to family, but I kept trying. I don't recall at the time, but my mother sat me down and said that I was too strict on my kids and that I needed to loosen my grip a little. I didn't understand why she said that, but I tried to lighten up. I was a single mom with two children working a ten-hour shift at night. In my mind there are the parenting type and the nurturing type. I was definitely the parenting type. I had become a robot in some ways. I was on a mission to teach my kids the tools they needed to survive in life. I had to provide and keep them safe. That is what I did day in and day out. I ran like clockwork and did anything to keep me moving. There were days where I would just cry and cry because I felt like a failure. I felt like I would never amount to anything. I would have flashbacks of so many things that have happened to me. I could count the dark spots all over my body. I felt like a wounded soul. I didn't know who to talk to. Who could help me? Shake it off Tamela you are a soldier. Get back to your mission. You are tough and strong. Push those feelings to the side and move on soldier. That's just what I did until I kept noticing those dark spots were not going away. Never let them see that you are weak. That's what I would tell myself. So, I would pick myself up and push everything to that place in my mind and lock it up. This was a revolving door in my mind. There are times in your life that you won't have closure to things. The hardest thing to do is except it and move on. I felt strong at times. I fled from an abusive marriage. I couldn't save myself, but I could save my children. Yes, I am good and there is nothing wrong with me. I am just fine.

FAIRYTALE

I once knew a girl who was full of life
She had no pain, no tears, and no spite
Her heart spoke to her one too many times
She finally got caught up in the storybook rhymes
She fell in love with a man that she thought was her
Destiny, but shortly after marriage,
It really wasn't meant to be
Seven years later she still waits for her story, but
Only God all mighty can give her the glory
If her mother had only told her the truth about life
The girl might have landed a nice shinning knight

CHAPTER VI

As time went on, I was starting to settle in Virginia. I was working and providing, but things still felt off. The pain, the hurt, the sadness, the nightmares, and the depression was still there. No matter what I did I couldn't get away from it. So, I did the only thing I knew to do. I would cry, write, and internalize my feelings. No one understands me anyway so why bother. Honestly, I didn't have much of a social life so getting to know people and dating was very foreign and scary to me, but I knew I had to find something to redirect my time and mind. Eventually, I did start dating someone. He was sixteen years younger than me. I know you are probably saying I was a cougar, but I was not. He showed me things I never knew was possible. I didn't know what it felt like to be respected and treated with so much love and kindness. I actually saw myself relaxing a lot just trying to embrace it. I never saw the age; I just saw the person and how he made me feel. I still had my moments of crying, dark nights, and triggers of my past, but I was hopeful, and I wanted to be happy. It felt weird to be in a relationship with no violence and no abuse. So, I took a chance and got married again. Now, marring someone that many years younger there is always a chance of things happening which it did, but it was never anything that made me feel threatened for my life or my kid's life. As time went on, we eventually divorced and still to this day we consider each other family. I learned a lot in that marriage but must of all I learned that there are different types of love. I also learned that I could love a woman just as hard as I could love a man. It's funny I never Identified myself in the past as one or the other because in my eyes it's just me. I like what I like no matter a person's sex, gender, race, etc. I'm laughing because I guess I let that little secret out. Some people call it being confused. I call it being me and choosing to be happy.

    The one thing about life, you have to expect the unexpected. The second divorce, I had to learn to love myself all over again. Basically, from the age of 20 to 41, I was married. So. dating and just being aware of what is in the current I was so behind. I had no social media of any kind. I wasn't old fashion by any means. I just wasn't up with the times. It was kind of funny. I was never big on technology or keeping up with what's going on. I always kind of rocked to my own beat. It was safer that way.

GEMINI

I try very hard, but no one pays attention

I cry very hard, but no one cares to listen

Each day of the week I feel like the 4 Seasons

Summer, Autumn, Winter, and Spring

Why is that such a terrible thing?

I can't begin to tell you all the hopes and

Dreams I have of living and

Becoming rich and never reentering my past

God knows, I try with all glory and shame

Through thick and thin and heartache and pain

My devotion to you

Is something that will never change

CHAPTER VII

Rocking to your own beat, sometimes means embracing the different. In the world we live in today people shy away and ridicule the uncommon and unfamiliar. To me different is normal. My life became more challenging at the age of 38. I noticed my hair was falling out. It was literally disappearing, like vanishing in front of my eyes. I was wearing Lace Fronts and I noticed in between installations my hair was disappearing. There was no glue, no tugging or tension on my hair so to me it was definitely unexpected. I decided to make an appointment with a dermatologist. Looking in the mirror at myself in between my hair appointments cause my self-esteem to decline. I felt truly unattractive. I just knew that I would never be loved again. Who would love someone so unattractive? I was taught your hair is your crown.

The doctor was very kind and patient with the process. He cut a piece of my scalp and sent it off to be analyzed and I also started receiving injections in my scalp to try and stimulate my hair growth. My first session was 17 injections. 3 weeks later I received another injection and pictures were taken of my scalp. 6 weeks later I was called to come into the doctor's office. I never been so nervous in my life. So, in a nutshell my hair would never grow back. I was diagnosed with something called Scarring Scalp Disease. It is similar to scarring Alopecia, but different. I went on later to lose my eyebrows and eyelashes. I couldn't do anything but cry. I could tell that my doctor was sympathetic toward me. When he told me he was unfamiliar with my condition I knew this was going to be a life change for me. He gave me a prescription of $1200 to go to the beauty shops to get wig units. Something was better than nothing, right! I took the prescription and went to the local beauty stores and presented them with the prescription and they looked at me like I was crazy. They were unfamiliar with my prescription, and they didn't know how to apply it. They told me to buy the hair units myself and send my receipts to the insurance company for reimbursement.

It was becoming too complicated, so I just decided to buy the hair with my own money. I got pretty good at applying my own Lace Front Units, but I still felt unattractive and monstrous looking when I saw myself in the mirror. I was so ashamed and embarrassed to show anyone my hair without a wig. I wouldn't even remove my Lace Front unless I was home alone. My daughter would always say, "Mommy you are beautiful."

I would just cry and cry. Why me? Nobody in my family has this condition so why do I have it? I thought I could just wear wigs forever, but what man or woman would want me now, I would ask. I just didn't have the confidence anymore.

After going through a second divorce and losing my hair I had to do something to make me feel like me again. I eventually started modeling again at the age of 42. I had entered back into the world that saved me once before. I became an Eye Candy Model for a year. I had never been that type of model before. I was surprised to be chosen as such. I had to admit that it helped with my self-esteem, but not enough. I started to feel restricted and controlled so I eventually decided to let it go. I have always been a versatile and artistic person so when I was approached and offered a position from a local photographer, I was happy to oblige. The freedom to create art though photography was intriguing. Soon after I became the first Brand Ambassador for that particular company, I started doing print work which was something new to me. I began doing local fashion shows and slowly making a name for myself. Through all the excitement I still felt empty. I was still having triggers, severe depression, and feelings of insecurity with my looks because of my hair condition. My hair never became a problem for photoshoots or fashion shows because I tried very hard to make sure my hair was versatile. The one thing modeling did was allow me to be someone else besides myself. This is a crazy twist because I was truly different from the average woman, but the model in me people embraced. They did not question her much. It was easy to hide my pain and the void that consumed me inside....Modeling filled that void.

BROKEN GLASS

One day we will see

Two journeys coming together

I know it's hard, but

Unfinished words, unfinished sentences

And unfinished thoughts

Will it ever make sense?

Decisions, too many to count

One foot in front of the other

You walk very fast like you're on a mission

Just to realize unfinished words

Unfinished sentences, unfinished thoughts and

Unfinished journeys

CHAPTER VIII

As time went on, I started to accept the way I looked, but there was a part of me that wanted to be free. I made a promise to myself that when I turned 45 that I would reveal my condition to the world. This would be one of the hardest things for me to do. The year 2020 turned out to be an amazing year. I went on a date with an amazing man. Well, I had known him in the industry for a couple of years. He was a fashion designer. He would always ask me to walk in his fashion shows, but I always had something else going on. Then finally I did walk in one of his shows. It was my first outside fashion show, and it was hot as hell that day. He was so attentive to everyone to make sure that we were comfortable. That's when I actually noticed how cute he was. A couple of months later he asked me out and that was the beginning of a fairy tale romance. That's when I realized I didn't have a type anymore. My type is how a person treats me and makes me feel. I began to learn how to love myself more. I knew this relationship was something special when I showed my true self with no hair, and he told me that I was beautiful. No one had ever told me that I was beautiful or at least not in a way that I believed it. That day I looked in the mirror and saw myself for the first time and I cried. I was ready to show the world the new me. The beautiful me.

Our romance blossomed. We did fashion shows together. He was always creating. He was such a Visionaire. It was time for my photo shoot for my 45th birthday and I was ready. I was so nervous that I had panic attacks, headaches, and my stomach was in knots. I was so fidgety and scared. The photoshoot actually turned out amazing! I never felt so invigorated before in my life. Laughing to myself, I just kept smiling. I drove all the way home with the sunroof open! Sun and wind beaming down on my bald head. Lol! Doing this year of 2020, we were dealing with a pandemic. Covid 19 was attacking the world and killing so many people. It was a very scary time. This virus was highly contagious and dangerous. The world as we knew it had changed forever. It was like living in a real-life horror story. It was time…June 20, 2020, at midnight, I posted my birthday pictures with no hair on social media. There was no turning back. I hit the send button! The response was overwhelming. I received nothing but positive and encouraging feedback. I was so grateful and humble. On my actual birthday I received a phone call from the CEO of a reputable magazine company to be featured on the cover and to share my story. I screamed and cried when I ended the phone call. God had just revealed to me that I was going to be alright.

    I was still battling PTSD and depression, but I was trying to work on my mental health. Two months after my birthday, I was having heart issues. I went to the emergency room thinking it was a reaction to my heart medicine I was taking. They gave me a Covid test in which was done by swabbing deep inside each nostril. They also gave me nitroglycerin for my heart and once my vitals were good, they sent me home. Two days later I received a phone call from the hospital stating that I tested positive for Covid 19. My boyfriend at the time was also positive. To say I was shocked was an understatement. I was so nervous because of my heart condition. There were so many reports of people dying with preexisting heart and breathing issues. I was determined to beat the odds. My triggers were on 1,000. I started having more triggers about the abuse I had endured in my first marriage. The nightmares were horrific. I would wake up crying along with head and body sweats. I would close my eyes and I saw myself fighting not to take my last breath. What's going on with me? I had no clue. A few weeks later I was diagnosed with severe PTSD on all levels. Crazy all these years I never told anyone. I was taught that you don't tell doctors things that can put you in a crazy house or a psychiatric ward. But I had a praying mother. She prayed for me day and night. Talking to my therapist and psychiatrist was a great benefit. Strangely, Covid also showed me what matters in life. The world truly showed their true colors.

Life is funny. You can waste it or enjoy every moment of it.

Things were looking up. My personal life was amazing. My therapy and medications were paying off in some ways. More brighter days I enjoyed. My boyfriend surprised me with an upcoming resort trip to Cove Haven in the Poconos Mountains. It was very romantic and beautiful there. On our second day there, my boyfriend proposed to me. I was in total shock but elated at the same time. He even dropped the ring because he was so nervous. Lol! The resort was amazingly beautiful, but there was something in my soul that just wasn't sitting right with me. On our way home my heart grew heavy, but I didn't know why. Less than 3 weeks later, God showed me. My fiancé had transitioned to the other side. I was totally devastated and heartbroken. I felt an emptiness that I did not know was possible. My world stopped that day. I didn't understand. Why is this happening? A part of me left with him. I was numb and done with love. Now what?

SUICIDE

A few days ago, I was almost at the end
My heart felt pain, but
Yet it felt so empty
I turned to my savior on my knees
As I slowly cried out for help!
Can he hear me I wonder?
Will he answer me
I begged, with one hand still and the other wild
I gripped the steel razor

I cried and I cried.
I felt pain and energy all at once, but
Yet I still diced and sliced at the hand that lay still
If it wasn't for a knock at the door
Where would I be?
Even though I was almost at the end
I still have the pain of loneliness,
Emptiness, and worthlessness
I don't know what the future beholds, but
I hope peace is mine

RAGE

On this day I lost my soul

To whom and what I did not know

My rage broke through like a knife in a cape, but

Who's to say today

The hurt blinded me 19 times fold

I couldn't let the story be untold

Why oh why did the goat cross the road

Especially,

When there was a truck coming with speed

To be knocked over indeed.

But what's the word I'm trying to say

Is unleash this beast today!

WANTING LOVE

There was a time when

I thought love was something you feel, but

Love for me is something that isn't real

I felt the hurt one too many times

In every way it's made me blind

Am I alive in this world with needs and thoughts?

Or am I just struggling for nothing, and

I just lost the fought

I've heard of jail, prison, and even the penitentiary, but

What is it like in my mind?

Yeah, I know you don't know what to call it

I just sink deeper and deeper until there is no more of it

I know what I want

I know what I need

But everything I feel only I believe

The one person in the world that I want to believe in me

And love me doesn't

I struggle for passion and love everyday

I feel like I'm pushed aside in everyway

Talented and having faith that I will make it one day

With or without, I still feel astray

Do I wait and hope for my love to thicken,
Or do I roll over
And cry and just keep dreaming?

CHAPTER IX

Mental health is real. So many times, we push or dismiss our feelings. Suck it up they say. Pray about it. It's all in your head. We don't go to doctors and tell our business. What will the Jones think? You will be okay. I have heard this on several occasions throughout my life. My conclusions are that they are false! My triggers are real. My depression is real. My paranoia is real. My suicidal thoughts are real. My anxiety is real. My self-isolation is real. My nightmares are real.

People would say that I am cheery, happy, and bubbly, which I am, but inside I am torn. Who could I talk to? Who would listen without judgment? Domestic violence was like living a day-to-day nightmare. Thirteen years of surviving domestic abuse, your mentality becomes a robot, and your thoughts are not your thoughts anymore. When will it end? When will I feel normal? When will have peace.? Will I ever be free.

I was diagnosed with Post Traumatic Stress Disorder (PTSD), service related through the military. Having a support system made a big difference in how I felt about life. Going to therapy and undergoing other treatments have helped me in so many ways. Learning how to talk about traumas and allowing myself to feel and grieve has been an important process of my treatment. Years of suppressing my feelings and emotions is definitely not healthy. I will never find the answers to the why, but I will have the answers to cope. I made a promise to myself to always be open and allow myself to live free. After two failed marriages and the transition of my last fiancé, I decided to close that chapter in my life. A little after my PTSD diagnosis, I was also diagnosed with early Alzheimer's Disease. I was truly surprised by that diagnosis, but so many things pointed in that direction that it was no denying it. Being educated on any medical condition is always important. Months prior to this, there were many signs of unusual thinking, confusion, memory loss, misplacing things, the lack of focus and not being able to complete easy tasks. My comprehension of simple things was off. I would get so frustrated and irritated with myself because I didn't know what was going on with me. So, to have an answer was welcomed. Now I can work on the treatment. Life has a way of throwing you curve balls and making you see what is important to you. It is time to continue living as best as I can and show the world, Gemini VI!

PTSD

I fell to my knees

Crying and begging God please

Take away the noise and

Terror in my mind

Stagnant and dilemmas

From the torment of my time

Too paranoid to fight

Too weak to stand

Gutted like a fish

While I reach for his hand

Count to 10 to calm my nerves they say

1 Mississippi, 2 Mississippi, show me the way

20 milligrams of Buspirone puts me in a daze

Enough to quiet my brain

And lighten my pain

Philippians 4:13

I can do all things through Christ which strengthens me

CHAPTER X

I have always viewed myself as a free spirit. The butterfly, the open-minded Gemini that loves with no limitations. To go through life being misunderstood, feeling confused and never feeling like I totally fit. But then you begin to notice things in yourself that needs to be awakened and set free. As long as I can remember, I have always had an attraction to women, but I was one that could love anything, a man, a woman, a tree, a dog, or a rock. As silly as it may sound, it is my reality. It's funny, now in today's society, they refer to what I am as pansexual. This means that I am not limited to a sexual choice with regards to biological sex, gender, or identity. I love who I love. I never really hid that part of my life. I just never had the opportunity to explore it.

After going through 2 marriages and several engagements, I have always been 100 percent honest and transparent with my mates about my sexuality. My mother, sister and daughter were always aware of my sexuality, but it wasn't until losing my fiancé in 2020 and then dealing with life altering health issues that I decided to be who I truly am and live for me.

The one thing about this world is that it is always evolving. Acceptance from the world can be something that I may never live to see, but acceptance of myself is the most important thing in fulfilling self-happiness.

So, this year I took a chance on me because I never really pursued the opposite sex. I am determined to find out and explore what happiness means to me.

Before the year ended in 2021, I met this amazing and beautiful woman on social media. I was very open minded to the friendship and getting to know someone again. To unapologetically be yourself with someone is the most amazing feeling in the world. In all my years I have never felt so natural and normal with someone. To have someone love you unconditionally, understand my different personalities, accept my illnesses, protect my heart and lift me up spiritually is truly rare.

I have to pinch myself to make sure she's real. When I met this woman, I saw us as the same, but yet different. She has been such an amazing light in my life. I love freely and openly in my heart with her. I thank God for my trials, tribulations, and testimonies. It took a lifetime for me to get here. Here is where I'll stay. I will continue to battle and fight for my mental health.

God is in control. One thing for sure, love this time, feels different...

> *To know me*
>
> *Is to love me*
>
> *My story*
> *Is my glory*
>
> *What you see*
>
> *Is the spirit in me*

I am me and I am free.
The Sixth One was released!

Gemini VI!

AWAKENING

The journey started so many years ago,
Feeling full of strife and needing to let go.
So much to say and so much to pray
I didn't do anything
The pressure to be me
Back and forth I glide
Trying not to show *my other side*
Who's going to pay *attention* without redemption
To that SOLDIER hiding in the trees
Patiently *a waiting* to finally breathe
The war within yourself
Makes you fight like hell
Chasing life for that *fairytale*
Look into my eyes and straight into my soul
What do you see?
It is the *Gemini* being set free
Broken Glass, reflections of my face
Deep in my heart I yearn for that embrace
My faith and hope rise high up above
As I desperately seek out *wanting love*

The time is here
There is nothing else to hide
I opened up my eyes
I have arrived

Awakening

BONUS POEMS

A WHISPER

A touch of my spirit

The time has come, yes once again where we laugh

Or cry at the end

And fear or crave what's ahead

Vows of my soul hear my voice

I came to you to cry and rejoice

My love is so deep like a sword with a thrust

I feel the waves and stinging right through my bust

He makes my eyes shine and drift through the wind

Followed by sounds of his voice

Crawling up my skin

Our vows together, for each other is strong enough

To pull me through anything

And having faith is a must

When all is said and done and there is no more

I will be singing and praising new life

While dancing with our Lord

HUE

I been writing poems since I can remember

Those that read my poems always tell me

They are deep and dark

But what is dark?

Your lies, your infidelity, your stealing, your killing

Who are you to judge my feelings?

There is no one better than the woman of this earth

There is no one better

Than the woman that gives birth

God made man and woman to make this world grow

He loved each one of them

As he watched them below

But something went wrong with his species

We started falling to our knees and

Shedding tears at our feet

Asking our Lord why me

And most of the time it's not me its them

Those that we pray for and ask forgiveness

So, as you read this you take this with you

This is my world and what I see

God will judge you not me

HYPOCRITES

How can one be true and content with the soul?

If everybody in the past

Have kept secrets that haven't been told

How can the world live with so much betrayal?

We are not judging them

They are the only ones that have failed

The saddest thing that breaks my heart is when

One of my loved ones lies from the start

Why should you be given a chance

To back tract your story

Because I know in the end

God almighty always get the glory

DAUGHTER

She is beautiful as can be

She is a very special part of me

A beautiful smile and a warm heart

She's kind to everyone from the start

She came from my soul and part of my flesh

She loves to dance and be creative not like the rest

She has big brown eyes and dimples in her smile

I steal energy from her and try to show her style

She is a star

She is mine

She is my daughter

RACE

There is a quiet storm growing inside
I feel the thunder the rumble falling on me
Lifting me off the ground
Thump, thump, thump I feel my heart pound
Breaking free to be unshackled
Letting Gods Love and breath see me free
My insides feel tortured
Please help me
My mind wont rest
My brain still hurts
The demons of the past continue to lurk
I pray and pray in so many ways
To wake up normal for just one day
As time winds down and
Nothing is promised forever
Would you leave life feeling alive
And fulfilled or would you leave feeling dead?

DO YOU SEE ME

Bliss, happiness, frustration, determination

The goose bumps are back

The unsure of the next is here

Is this the right decision

Am I passing this test?

I am not sure

One day is okay

The next day it is not but that's life

The ying and the yang of everything

Everything is foreign

Everything is new yet familiar

They know me, but I don't know you

They smile and say it's been a long time, but

I'm not that little girl you knew

Nor am I that girl you see.

I'm just me

AUTHENTICLY ME

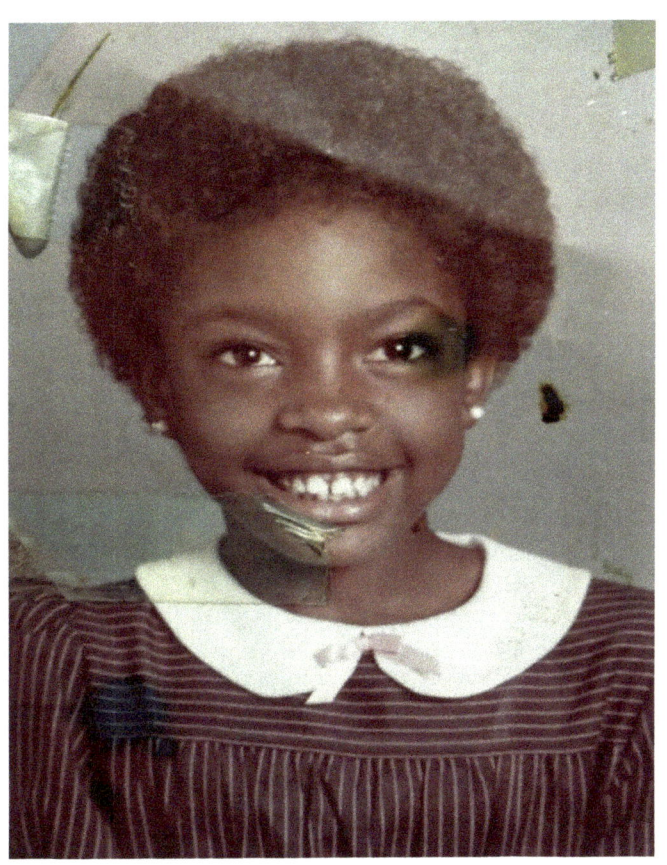

MY SINCERE ADVICE

Mental health awareness is very important. Do not be afraid to reach out for help. I suffered in silence for many years not knowing who to turn to and how to get help. Utilize your resources to become
The best version of you.

Thank you for taking the time out
To read my story.

Tamela D Carrington

www.ingramcontent.com/pod-product-compliance
Lightning Source LLC
Chambersburg PA
CBHW051700090426
42736CB00013B/2463